One day, as Brahma the Creator, was sitting in Satyaloka, He thought to himself.

"I am the Creator of the Universe. Why should Vishnu think that he is greater than me?"

So, H[...]

"O Vishnu[...] Creator of the Universe, and greater than you, consequently. So, you should worship me!"

"O Brahma! Remember that you were born from my navel. Besides, I am the one who preserves everything. So, I am greater!"

Thereupon the Gods began arguing...

"I am the greatest!"

"No! I am greater!"

Devas started talking to each other.

"Look! Lord Brahma and Lord Vishnu have begun fighting!"

"Let us go and tell Lord Shiva!"

All the Devas went to Kailasa.

"O Lord Shiva! Please help us. Lord Brahma and Lord Vishnu are quarrelling about who is greater!"

"All right! I shall go and settle their fight!"

The two Gods met.

"Look! Here is the Ketaki flower which adorns Shiva's head. It is proof that I found Shiva's head. So, I have won the test and am the greatest!"

"I give up! I could not find the base of the pillar or Shiva's feet! So, Shiva is greater than both of us!"

"O Ketaki! Is what Brahma says true - were you sitting on Shiva's head?"

"Of course it is true!"

Just then Lord Shiva appeared from the pillar of fire.

"What a great liar you are, Ketaki! You were not sitting on my head at all! How can you say other-wise! As a punishment, you shall not be used in my worship!"

With a wave of his hand, Shiva created a dreadful being.

"Bhairava! I order you to punish Brahma for having lied to me and to Vishnu about me!"

Bhairava immediately rushed forward and cut off one of Brahma's five heads.

Bhairava raised his sword to cut off another of Brahma's heads, when Brahma fell at Shiva's feet.

"O Lord Shiva! Please forgive Lord Brahma! I too failed in my attempt to reach the base of this pillar of fire to find your feet. So you are truly the greatest of us all!"

"Please forgive me for the great mistake I made!"

"Yes, O LORD OF LORDS! You are the Supreme Being!"

"O Lord Shiva! You are known for your compassionate and generous nature. Please forgive the Ketaki flower for its pride too!"

"All right! The Ketaki flower will be allowed to decorate the temple raised for my worship. But, Brahma will not be worshipped."

# 2. SHIVA AND SATI

Daksha Prajapati had sixteen beautiful daughters. His wife, Prasuti (who was the daughter of Manu) said -

"My Lord, the time has come to arrange for our daughters' marriages."

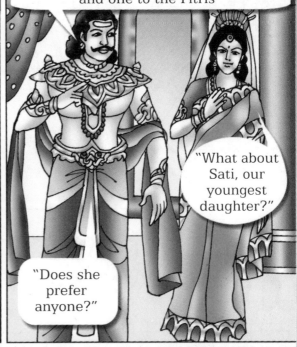

"We shall give thirteen of them in marriage to Dharma, and one to Agni and one to the Pitris"

"What about Sati, our youngest daughter?"

"Does she prefer anyone?"

"Sati is a strange girl. While others of her age love to play and dance, Sati prefers to sit and meditate on Shiva."

At that very moment, Narada appeared before Daksha Prajapati and Prasuti.

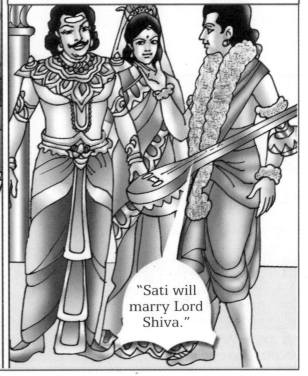

"Sati will marry Lord Shiva."

So, Daksha Prajapati and Prasuti gave their daughter, Sati, in marriage to Lord Shiva.

Some time later, the great Brahma Satra yagnya was being performed by Marichi and other famous rishis.

All the devas, rishis and other denizens of the heavens were present.

As the yagnya began, there was a sudden commotion and all eyes turned to the entrance.

The imposing figure of Daksha Prajapati strode in. Everyone got up and bowed respectfully. Only two remained seated.

Daksha Prajapati went to seek the blessings of his father, Lord Brahma - who had remained seated.

"Just look at that arrogant ash-smeared son-in-law of mine! He has not even acknowledged my presence! I shouldn't have given my Sati to this beggar!"

As he sat down, he thought,

"I must teach him a lesson! I shall conduct a greater yagnya to which all shall be invited but my boorish son-in-law!"

His daughter, Sati, who was the wife of Lord Shiva, saw the stream of devas, rishis and kings going towards her father's house.

"What is the matter?"

"O Sati Devi! Your father, Daksha Prajapati is performing a very great yagnya!"

Sati at once went to her husband.

"My Lord, I have just heard that my father, Daksha Prajapati, is performing a great yagnya. Please let us go! I wish to see my mother and sisters!"

Shiva looked at Sati with a sad smile on his face.

"My beloved wife! Your father has not invited us. He regards me as his chief enemy as he thinks that I insulted him. Do you remember that everyone present at the Brahma Satra yagnya performed by Marichi and other rishis, stood up when he entered? But I did not bow to him. Your father, Daksha Prajapati, has become too arrogant and has spoken ill of me in the presence of all. He has even cursed me - that I should not receive the offerings of the yagnya. So, no good will come if you go to Daksha's yagnya. He will not respect you!"

Sati listened to all this with a downcast face.

"A daughter doesn't have to be invited - she is free to go to her father's house! I know that my Lord is most unwilling to let me go! What shall I do?"

Sati walked up and down restlessly, at last she came to a decision.

Sati thought and prepared to leave Kailasa.

"I will go to my father's yagnya!"

Shiva watched her. But He could not prevent Sati. He sent His army of ganas, headed by Nandi, to escort His wife to Daksha's yagnyasala.

Daksha Prajapati ignored Sati when she entered the yagnyasala.

"How can uninvited people come here?"

Sati's anger rose when she heard these cruel words from her own father.

Sati sat down in a yogic pose and prayed to Agni, the God of Fire, to enter her. And, while everyone watched helplessly, Sati was soon reduced to a small pile of ashes.

"My Lord warned me that I would be treated badly if I came, but I did not listen to Him! I was foolish to think that my father would welcome me! I am ashamed to be called your daughter! You shall pay for your insult to my Lord! I shall be reborn to a father whom I can respect - what is the use of living anymore?"

"Sati is dead! Cruel Daksha! He will have to face Shiva's wrath!"

Shiva was furious when he heard what had occurred at Daksha's yagnyasala. He plucked handful of His hair and flung them on the ground. A terrible figure appeared.

These cries reached the ears of Shiva's attendants. They rushed back to Kailasa to tell Shiva what had happened.

"Veerabhadra! Go and destroy Daksha at once!"

Led by the terrible Veerabhadra, Shiva's hordes descended on Daksha's yagnyasala and laid it waste in seconds. All those who had insulted Sati met with severe punishment. Veerabhadra sought out Daksha and strangled him. He severed Daksha's head from his body and flung it into the sacrificial fire.

The survivors went to Lord Brahma and Lord Vishnu who had not attended Daksha's yagnya and told them all that had happened.

"We shall all go to Lord Shiva and beg for mercy!"

They all went to Kailasa and bowed to Lord Shiva.

"O Lord! Be merciful and restore Daksha to life so that he can complete the yagnya!"

"Daksha had to be taught a lesson as he became too proud! I am not angry with him! Bring me the head of the sacrificial goat and I shall fit it to Daksha's body."

This was done and Daksha was restored to life.

"Please forgive me for having insulted You, Lord Shiva! I was blind to Your true greatness! I weep for my dear daughter!"

# 3. A SURPRISE FOR SHIVA

Once there was a wicked asura called Bhasmasura.

"I wish to become powerful and brave, and defeat all the devas! How shall I go about it?"

Just then Narada appeared before him.

"O great sage! Please tell me how I can become powerful!"

"Do penance to Lord Shiva and get a boon from Him!"

So, Bhasmasura worshipped Lord Shiva who finally appeared before him.

"I bless you for your devotion! Ask me for any boon!"

"O Lord Shiva! I wish to become all powerful! Please grant me the boon that anyone's head I touch with my right hand should be reduced to ashes at once!"

"So be it!"

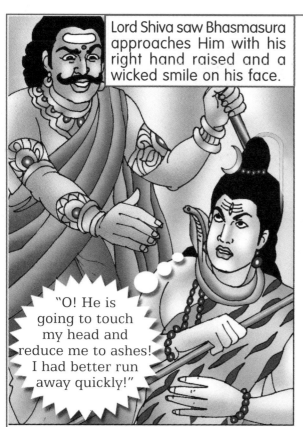

Lord Shiva saw Bhasmasura approaches Him with his right hand raised and a wicked smile on his face.

"O! He is going to touch my head and reduce me to ashes! I had better run away quickly!"

Shiva ran for His life. Bhasmasura ran after Him.

"I will pray to Lord Vishnu to save me"!

"O Lord Vishnu, I am in a great trouble. Kindly save me!"

"O! Lord Shiva is in great trouble! I had better help Him!"

Vishnu changed His form and appeared as a beautiful woman before Bhasmasura.

"What is your name, beautiful one?"

"I am called Mohini! You look tired! Why are you running?"

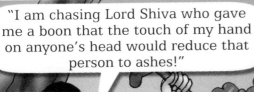

"I am chasing Lord Shiva who gave me a boon that the touch of my hand on anyone's head would reduce that person to ashes!"

"What a silly thing to believe! Lord Shiva's words cannot be trusted! Why don't you put your hand on your own head and see?"

Bhasmasura stared at Mohini.

"All right! I shall test Shiva's words on myself and see if His boon works!"

He raised his right hand and placed it on his head.

At once there was a loud roar and Bhasmasura was reduced to ashes!

She vanished before His eyes and reappeared as Lord Vishnu.

"Thank you for saving me, beautiful one!"

"Be more careful when You give boons in future!"

# 4. THE MARRIAGE OF SHIVA AND PARVATI

King Himavan ruled over the sacred Himalayas. His wife, Mena Devi, was blessed with a baby girl who was none other than the Goddess Sati now reborn as Parvati.

One day, sage Narada appeared before King Himavan and Queen Mena Devi.

"When your daughter reaches marriageable age, she will wed Lord Shiva!"

From that day, Parvati began worshipping Lord Shiva with great devotion.

Now, Parvati become a beautiful young woman.

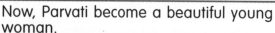

"Father, I wish to serve Lord Shiva. Please let us go and see Him!"

Himavan took Parvati to Kailasa where Lord Shiva was in deep meditation.

"O Lord Shiva! This is my daughter, Parvati. She is intensely devoted to You and wishes to serve You. Please grant her desire!"

After the tragic death of Sati, Lord Shiva did not permit any woman to serve Him.

"O King Himavan! You are aware that I have cut myself off from all earthly desires. Do you still think that it is right for me to accept your daughter's services?"

Parvati folded her hands respectfully and said.

"O Lord Shiva! Please permit me to serve You! I shall not get in your way at all!"

"As you sincerely wish to serve me, I agree!"

Parvati began serving her Lord with devotion.

"I shall somehow marry Lord Shiva!"

At that time, the devas were being greatly harassed by a fierce asura called Tarakasura.

A long time ago, Tarakasura had performed penance to Lord Brahma.

Tarakasura knew that after the death of Sati, Shiva had become a hermit.

"O Lord Brahma! Please grant me the boon of invincibility. No one should be able to defeat me, but Lord Shiva's son!"

"So be it!"

Protected by Brahma's boon, Tarakasura became even more powerful and wicked. The devas could stand it no longer and went to Satyaloka.

"O Brahma! Please protect us from Tarakasura!"

"I cannot do anything as Tarakasura obtained a boon from me that only Lord Shiva's son should be able to defeat him. The asura knows that after Sati's death, Lord Shiva will not marry again!"

"Is there any way out?"

"There is only one way out and that is to make Lord Shiva marry somehow! The son born of this marriage will defeat Tarakasura!"

The devas and the rishis all went to see Manmatha, the God of Love.

"Please can you make Lord Shiva change His mind and heart so that he will marry and beget a son?"

"I am ready to do whatever I can for the welfare of the world, even if I lose my life in the attempt!"

Manmatha, accompanied by his wife, Rati Devi, went to the place where Shiva sat in meditation. Parvati was making floral garlands some yards away.

'The time is ripe for me to act!'

Shiva felt a change in the atmosphere - a cool scented breeze blew and the birds chirped happily. At that moment Manmatha shot an arrow from his sugarcane bow to compel Shiva to look at Parvati who was nearby.

Shiva opened His eyes and saw Manmatha.

"How dare you disturb me?"

A flash of fire streamed out and reduced Manmatha to a heap of ashes.

Rati Devi wept bitterly as she went to Amaravati and told Indra what had happened.

"Please help me!"

"I shall go to see Lord Shiva!"

Indra and the other devas went to see Lord Shiva.

"Rati Devi will regain her husband one day when he is reborn as Lord Krishna's son. She has to be patient till then."

"Please help Rati Devi!"

Parvati had seen what had happened and was filled with sadness.

'I shall go to another place to perform penance. But I am still determined to marry Lord Shiva!'

She went to another jungle and resumed her worship of Lord Shiva.

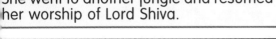

In the meantime, Tarakasura's atrocities grew worse and all the devas went to Kailasa.

"O Lord Shiva! Please save us from the wicked Tarakasura. He has obtained a boon from Lord Brahma that only your son can kill him!"

"Indra, you know that I have given up all desires and will not be able to concentrate on meditation if a woman enters my life! Who will marry me?"

"O Lord Shiva! You are the refuge of the world! And only you can save mankind!"

"O Lord Shiva! You are aware that Parvati has been performing penance to marry you!"

"All right! I agree!"

'I must test Parvati's devotion to me!'

Lord Shiva sent for the 'Sapta rishis'*.

"Go and try to persuade Parvati not to marry me. Speak slightly of me and let us see what happens!"

* Seven sages

The rishis went to the place where Parvati was meditating.

"O beautiful maiden! Why are you wasting your time by worshipping Lord Shiva? You are a princess and are used to live a life of luxury."

"O learned ones! I have decided to marry no one but Lord Shiva!"

The rishis told Shiva what had happened.

"I myself shall test Parvati's resolve to marry me."

He went disguised as an old man to Parvati. She welcomed Him with respect.

"O respected one, why are you wandering in this jungle where fierce animals dwell? It is not safe for you!"

"Thank you for your kind concern. But why are you living here alone? It is not safe for you too! Who are you?"

"I am Parvati, the daughter of King Himavan and Queen Mena Devi. I am doing penance here to marry Lord Shiva and shall stay here till I achieve my desire!"

"Why are you thinking of ruining your life by this strange desire? Lord Shiva does not deserve such devotion from you!"

"O Aged! It is out of respect for your age that I am speaking gently to you. Please do not talk ill of Lord Shiva - He is my chosen Lord and I shall marry Him and no one else!"

Lord Shiva then revealed His true form.

"I shall marry you soon, as you have pleased me by your sincere devotion!"

Parvati continued her devoted service to Lord Shiva as they lived happily in Kailasa.

Soon, King Himavan and Queen Mena Devi celebrated Parvati's marriage to Lord Shiva with great pomp.

21

Tarakasura continued with his deeds of terror. He had forgotten the words of Brahma who had said, `As you desire, only a son born to Lord Shiva will be able to defeat you.'

There was great rejoicing in Kailasa as Goddess Parvati had given birth to a baby boy.

"We shall call him Subramanya."

"O mighty Tarakasura! Have you heard the news? Lord Shiva has become the father of a son!"

"I must think of ways to get rid of my new opponent!"

"I know that Tarakasura will try to harm my son, so, I shall bestow great powers on him!"

Lord Shiva too gave him divine weapons.

Tarakasura sent an army of his strong asuras to kill young Subramanya. But the divine child was protected by his parents' powerful astras and killed the asuras easily.

"O Tarakasura! Your mighty army has been defeated by Shiva's son!"

"What! I will go and fight with him myself!"

All the devas, led by Indra, gathered to watch the battle between Subramanya and Tarakasura.

At last, Subramanya shot a divine astra at Tarakasura and killed him.

The devas showered flowers on Subramanya, glad to be rid of the asura!

23

# 5. WHY SHIVA HAS A BLUE THROAT

The devas and the asuras churned the Ocean of Milk, the `AMRITAMANTHANA`.

"We shall use Mount Mandara and ask Vasuki to be the 'rope' that can be held and pulled at both ends."

"It will be beneath our dignity to hold the tail of the snake!"

"All right! we shall hold the tail while you can pull the head!"

Churning began; after some time, the deadly poison, HAALAHAALA, emerged from Vasuki's mouth. As it spread over the entire universe, many of the devas and asuras fell unconscious.

The devas prayed to Lord Shiva.

"O Lord of Lords! You are our saviour! The entire universe is affected by the deadly HAALAHAALA! Please save us!"

"Do not worry! I always protect my devotees!"

He took the HAALAHAALA poison in His palms and drank it.

Just then, Parvati came rushing up and placed her hand around Shiva's throat.

"O Lord! Please let the poison remain in your throat. Do not swallow it!"

The poison remained in Shiva's throat, staining the white neck of the Lord with blue. That is why Lord Shiva is also known as 'Neelakanta'.

# 6. SHIVA TEACHES GANGA A LESSON

Bhagiratha of the Ikshvaku line had a great desire.

"I must bring the Ganga down from heaven to earth and so give salvation to my ancestors, the 60,000 sons of King Sagara who were burnt to ashes by the rishi Kapila. I will perform penance to please Ganga."

At last Ganga appeared before him.

"Please, Mother Ganga! I wish to secure salvation for my ancestors. They have not obtained it though three generations of my line have passed. The great rishi, Kapila said that only you can save them."

"I will be glad to help you. But, Bhagiratha, you do not know with what great speed I will flow down to earth. Who is there powerful enough to break my fall? If my descent is not stopped, I will flow straight down to Patalaloka and your penance will be wasted. In any case, why should I leave Swargaloka and come down to sinful earth where I will be defiled?"

"O Mother Ganga! Great rishis who forever think of Narayana will bathe in you and keep you pure. I will pray to Lord Shiva to help me to solve the problem of your descent to earth!"

"So be it! Lord Shiva will be powerful enough to bear my descent!"

Bhagiratha began to perform penance again. This time it was to please Lord Shiva who appeared before His devotee.

"What can I do for you, Bhagiratha?"

"So be it!"

"O Lord Shiva! My ancestors were reduced to ashes for displeasing the great Kapila. He told my grandfather that their souls would be purified only if Ganga came to earth and washed their ashes. I prayed to Mother Ganga who has agreed if You took on your head her downward journey to earth."

All the devas watched as Ganga began her descent, and Lord Shiva stood upright to receive her in His matted locks. But she was very arrogant and sped as fast as she could, hoping to defeat Shiva.

A strange thing happened. The Ganga flowed into Shiva's matted locks, but not a drop of her water trickled out!

"Please Lord Shiva! Have pity on me and release Ganga!"

Shiva allowed a chastened Ganga to flow from His locks and flow down to earth. He had taught Mother Ganga a lesson in humility.

# 7. A BLESSING IN DISGUISE

Once a hunter was roaming about in a forest. He was a very cruel man but was greatly attached to his family.

"Darkness is about to fall and I still haven't killed a single animal. How shall I feed my hungry family? I will climb this tree and spend the night out of reach of wild animals!"

The hunter climbed the tree and moved about to perch more comfortably on a high branch.

"I will have to go hungry as I have no food! I shall have to keep awake the whole night in case I fall off the tree. So, I will pluck the leaves of the tree and drop them one by one!"

The hunter did not know that it was a Bilva tree on which he was sitting. Or that he had unknowingly scattered Bilva leaves on a Shivalinga which was at the foot of the tree.

After some time, a deer came up. The hunter raised his bow to take aim. The deer saw the hunter. More leaves fell as the hunter moved.

"O hunter! Please do not kill me as yet! I will go home to bid my family goodbye and come back soon!"

The hunter felt sorry for the deer and let it go.

Some time passed and another deer came into view. The hunter raised his bow to shoot it. Once again more Bilva leaves fell on the Shivalinga below the tree as he moved. The deer saw the hunter.

"O hunter! Please let me go home to say goodbye to my family. I promise to come back soon!"

'This deer is saying the same thing as the first deer said! How much they love their families!'

"All right! You may go. But, come back soon!"

Daylight would be breaking soon. The hunter heard a noise and looked down after some time.

'Why! Both the female deer have come back with their families!'

On reaching the tree, the male deer looked up.

"O hunter! Please kill me instead of my mates!"

"No, no! take our lives, kill us; how can we live without our parents?"

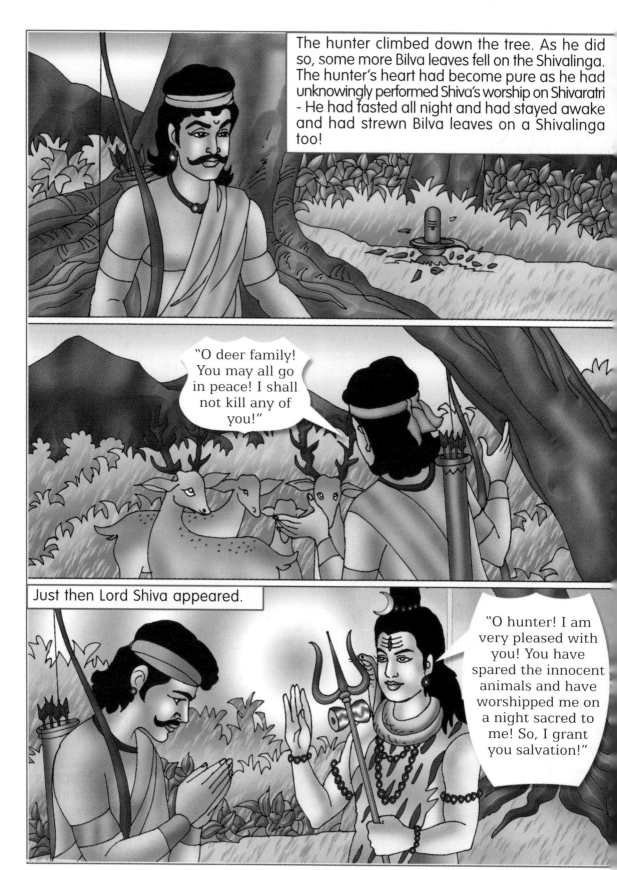

The hunter climbed down the tree. As he did so, some more Bilva leaves fell on the Shivalinga. The hunter's heart had become pure as he had unknowingly performed Shiva's worship on Shivaratri - He had fasted all night and had stayed awake and had strewn Bilva leaves on a Shivalinga too!

"O deer family! You may all go in peace! I shall not kill any of you!"

Just then Lord Shiva appeared.

"O hunter! I am very pleased with you! You have spared the innocent animals and have worshipped me on a night sacred to me! So, I grant you salvation!"

# 8. SHIVA AND ARJUNA

The Pandavas were spending their exile in the forest after they lost their kingdom to the Kauravas. Veda Vyasa came to see them and advised Arjuna.

"O Arjuna! Do penance to Lord Shiva and obtain the powerful 'PASHUPATA' astra from Him!"

He whispered a mantra into Arjuna's ear.

"Repeat this mantra with devotion in a secluded forest!"

Arjuna went to meditate in a forest. He made a Shivalinga and began chanting the mantra.

One day a boar came running up.

'It is disturbing my concentration!'

'I shall kill it with my Gandiva*!'

He took up his bow and strung an arrow.

*Arjuna's famous bow

At the same time, Shiva and Parvati came to the forest disguised as a hunter and his wife to test Arjuna. Shiva too shot an arrow at the boar at the same moment as Arjuna did.

Both of them began fighting.

Lord Shiva was pleased with the bravery Arjuna displayed. He revealed His true form.